Digital Habits

5 Simple Tips to Help Keep You and Your Information Safe Online

Something More Publishing
Kingston, New York 12401
Printed in the United States

DIGITAL
HABITS

5 SIMPLE TIPS TO HELP KEEP YOU AND YOUR INFORMATION SAFE ONLINE

David W. Schropfer

Something More Publishing
Printed in the USA
Charleston, South Carolina

Something More Publishing
Kingston, New York 12401

20 19 18 17 16 15 14
40 39 38 37 36 35 34 33 Pbk.

Schropfer, David W
Digital Habits: 5 Simple Tips to Help Keep You and Your Information Safe Online / David W. Schropfer

ISBN-13: 978-1535297998
ISBN-10: 1535297999

FOR MY CHILDREN

...and for yours.

Acknowledgements

My wife is my primary motivation, and perpetual inspiration. She is my first and last collaborator, and she is also my editor. No one else put in more work, displayed more patience, or contributed more to the creative spark and timely completion of this work.

Contents

Introduction

"Don't tug on Superman's cape, don't spit in the wind, don't pull the mask off the old Lone Ranger..."

-Jim Croce

Jim had to the right idea. The rules in his iconic song are certainly easy to follow!

But, they will not keep you safe from too many pitfalls or traps, primarily because they protect the listener from fictional characters.

The traps on the Internet are definitely not fictional, and the rules to keep you safe are anything but easy to follow. There are endless publications, blogs, and other articles telling you what not to do, how ***not*** to use the Internet, and warning you of all the worst-case scenarios that are possible in the digital world. Many of the articles on the topic of Internet security can be summarized something like this:

> *Trust nothing, verify everything, use a different password on every site, make every password at least as long as the Nile River, use letters, numbers, symbols, and ancient Egyptian hieroglyphics (requires a special keyboard), never write your password anywhere, and change all your passwords eight times a week (twice on Sundays).*

If you followed all of those rules to the letter, you would spend half of your Digital Life simply managing the rules, leaving you little time to actually USE your devices. The result would be to basically not access the Internet at all. For those of you who have read some of those publications, you know this is no exaggeration.

So, we can conclude fictitious traps = easy rules, and; Real traps = oppressively difficult rules.

It's time for a new approach. Simple, reasonable habits to replace many of the complex rules.

If you only adopt the first two simple habits of this book, you will have a substantially more enjoyable experience online. And, all 5 of these habits are designed to be easy to understand, and easy to follow.

This book is for anyone who wants to understand a few simple things they can do to avoid obvious traps and pitfalls in their Digital Life. The ideas expressed in this book will not keep you completely safe on the Internet or on a connected device, but no advice or product will keep you *completely* safe from the traps and pitfalls of the Internet, other than not using computers at all.

Most importantly, this book offers reason, and ~~even~~ logic, behind the habits it suggests. Each habit is specifically designed to help you navigate around a particular type of trap or risk on the Internet. If you want to understand more about those traps, and simple things you can do to make it more likely to avoid the traps, then this book is for you.

> Afraid of all of the viruses and scary traps online? This book is your ticket out of Internet Abstinence.

Eliminate Reason and Accountability

Did you do anything fun today?

If so, what did you do that you found to be fun? Maybe you got to hike up your favorite mountain trail, or jog your favorite street course. Maybe you had a chance to have a cup of coffee with old friends. Or perhaps you just found a few minutes to read a great book.

The definition of "fun" varies greatly from person-to-person, and that is exactly why you need to read this book. Because, the fact is, there are many, many people who find it "fun" to destroy other people's precious digital content, and disrupt the digital lives of others.

That's right, just for fun.

Many kinds of hacks and viruses offer NO financial gain. But, if the attacker is receiving no financial gain, are there any quasi-sane reasons other than just fun? Sure. These reasons run the gamut from the desire to make political statements, or as a form of activism, or perhaps to get "revenge" against a person that was forcibly removed from a Christmas card list. But, unless you were the person forcibly removed from the Christmas card list, you are probably not being specifically or personally targeted. Most hackers set traps for anyone to fall into. They attack people by the thousands, or hundreds of thousands, at a time. They generally are intentionally casting a wide net because they know that some of us will make a simple mistake that allows us to fall into that trap.

So, that means that traps you are most likely to fall victim to are set by one of two types of people who do malicious things with computers: Hackers and Thieves.

Hacker, or Attacker

The first type of hacker lays these traps because of a motivation that falls somewhere on the spectrum of 'fun' for them. It is illogical, and in some cases unimaginable, but it is true.

For the purpose of the book, the term 'Hacker' refers to malicious activity, not just "creative" activity. There are many types of activities that are really just creative ways of getting something done, but are technically considered 'hacks.'

An excerpt of the definition of 'hack' as it appears in the Merriam Webster dictionary:

> **hack**[i] verb \'hak\
>
> transitive verb definition: *To manage successfully*
>
> intransitive verb definitions: *a: to write computer programs for enjoyment. b: to gain access to a computer illegally*

The transitive verb is really meant for another context, such as, "He just couldn't hack the noise in his new neighborhood." But, the definition is perfect: *To manage successfully*. Even the intransitive verb definitions are not as accurate for a general definition of a hack. Computers and networks are complex things that are indispensable to the lives of many. And sometimes we just have to get things done.

Has your daughter ever successfully unlocked your iPhone because she wants to see the picture you took of her, and she guessed your passcode was 1111? That is a hack. Did your husband ever covertly unlock your laptop to read your contacts because he needed an email address to plan a surprise birthday party? That is a hack. Have you ever used a 'trick' from your neighbor to open your laptop after the screen froze? That's a hack.

There are many, many types of everyday hacks that are harmless, causing no meaningful damage to anybody. Importantly, with these "friendly" hacks, there's no malicious intent.

But, sadly, non-malicious hacks are neither newsworthy, not the focus of this book. It is the large and growing number of malicious hacks, both the people who have a non-financial motivation (but are willing to let you get caught in their 'protest') and the people that just enjoy malicious acts. We all have lots of names for the latter group, but in this book they will be called simply 'attackers' or just 'hackers.' Literally, there is no financial gain for them personally, the only gain the protest they think they have emphasized, or the harm that they caused. They're limited to bragging about their accomplishments in chat rooms on the Deep Web, they can never publicly admit to their deeds for fear of prosecution.

And they have no other credible reason, except fun.

Thieves

Now that we have dispensed with logic and reason, we can explore the other major category of hacker. Let's call them 'thieves.' These people don't just want to steal your money; sometimes they want to steal something of value from you other than money, such as using the computing power of your device as part of a network under someone else's control (a botnet), or force your laptop to help send millions of spam messages all over the world. In fact, there are many things of value, both financial and otherwise, that the thief wants to extract from your computer. For simplicity, these thieves ultimately have some financial gain from their theft; whether it's directly from your bank account or not. They will get paid by someone, somehow, for something their hack produces from your computer or mobile device.

So, the motive for thieves to hack your computer is financial gain. And, hacking for financial gain is the intent of the vast majority of malicious activity in the digital world. According to Hackmageddon.com[ii], one out of every three cyber attacks are motivated by Cyber Crime. Attacks for financial gain are somewhat more predictable than attacks for "fun" because we know what the thieves are after, and how to stop them.

Rational Or Irrational

The point is: a digital attack can be rational or irrational. Think about that.

As you read this book, you will learn about some types of attack, and *simple* habits you can use to avoid common traps. Just don't ask why the attacker does it. There may be logic to an attack, and there may not. An attack does not have to make sense and it does not have to target only the rich or powerful. An attack is simply a malicious act that uses a computer and a network.

Whether the attacker is motivated by financial gain, or to make a political statement, or just plain fun, the volume of these attacks is so high, and so common, that any user of any device on any network can be attacked. You don't need to be a world leader, or billionaire, or a corporate CEO to be the target of an attack. Attackers cast such a wide net that anyone can be caught. It's like putting a bear trap in a strip mall; the traps are designed to catch a large powerful prey, but it is much more likely to ensnare an innocent person passing by.

> Most online traps are like putting a bear trap in a strip mall; the traps are designed to catch a large powerful prey, but it is much more likely to ensnare an innocent person passing by.

And, unfortunately, there is no single thing you can do to defend yourself. There is no silver bullet. Safety and security is about layers - a combination of activities or habits that will protect you. And that is what this book is about- a few simple habits that will help you avoid the multitude of ongoing, random, rational and irrational attacks in the digital world.

No Rules

This book was (obviously) written by the author, but it was also written *for* the author. And, for people like the author. The fact is, we all hate rules. This is not a totally irrational position because there are many rules that are the mere whims of rule makers, and have no basis in fact.

Responsible adults should always ask, "why?" before following the rules. Some rules are pretty obvious, like, "Don't go swimming with a barbell." That's a good one; I respect that, and it doesn't need a lot of explanation.

Here's another one: If you eat a hotdog, don't go swimming. Why? Does it really take so much digestive activity after I eat a hot dog that my muscles are starved for blood and oxygen in such a way that I am unable to maintain buoyancy? I'm more skeptical about that one.

The structure of this book is intended to explain common known threats in the security industry that we are constantly working against. This book will not protect you from everything, but employing simple habits, and understanding why you are employing those habits, will help you easily avoid some of the common traps set for you on the Internet, and with connected devices.

Habits?

So, why habits, and not tasks? Because habits are behavioral, not technical. Habits are relatively easy things to do; and they have to be easy, otherwise you could not continue to do them on a regular basis. A "task" is how to reconfigure your WiFi, or how to set up backup disk, or how to set up an untraceable web browser. **You will find no tasks in this book, just simple, minor things to do (or avoid) every time you use a computer or mobile device.**

Here are some examples:

Do you understand your physical health? Of course you do. If you eat cake frosting for breakfast lunch and dinner, you won't feel good, eventually.

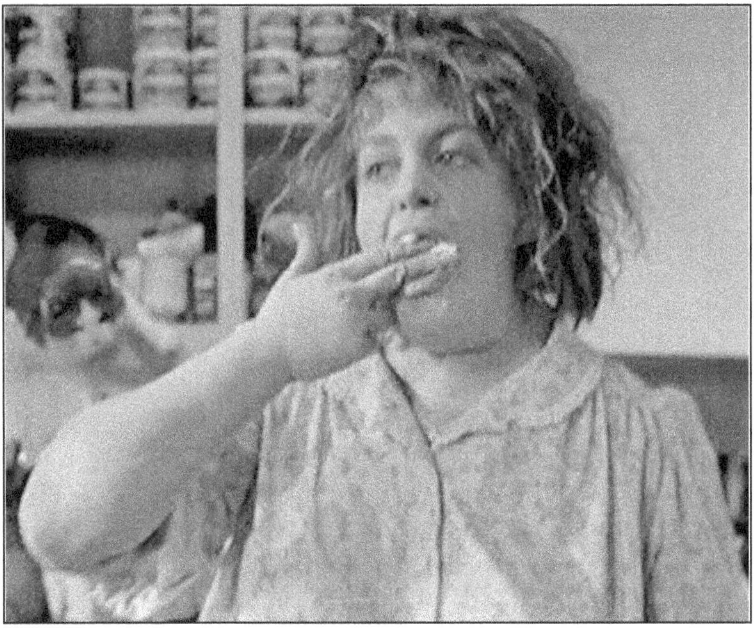

1: Goldie Hawn stars as the cake frosting-eating Helen Sharp in Universal Pictures' 1992 Movie, "Death Becomes Her"

That's why you have developed the habit of eating a combination of foods, not just the sugary, fatty stuff.

Do you understand your mental health? Of course you do. It would take virtually no effort to stare at a screen all day. You probably can command thousands of hours of video that would be entertaining to you with almost no effort at all. But, if you entertained yourself all day every day, you know that your mind would decay into a non-functioning lump of clay. So, you developed a habit of occasionally suspending your entertainment time for other activities, like time with loved ones, or work, or pursuit of your passion.

In both cases, the habit is easy, and the reward is great. Habits have to be easy so you can do them, everyday, or multiple times per day.

This same principle may be true for your financial life, your sex life, your professional life, etc. This principle is also true for your Digital Life; like anything else, you need healthy habits.

So, read on, adopt some simple new habits, and continue to enjoy your Digital Life.

Digital Habit 1:

SHUT THE FRONT DOOR

This habit may seem obvious, but it is also probably the element that most people neglect in the name of convenience. It is simply using the first layer of security that every device offers: require a password to turn it 'on.'

Have you ever seen the front door to a house without a lock on it? Probably not. Think of computers the exactly the same way.

Every computer and mobile device will allow you to set a password that must be entered before that device will function, or turn 'on.'. In other words, every time you turn the device on, or wake it up from 'Sleep' Mode, you will need to enter a password, or passcode, or (in some cases) a swipe of your finger, before you can use the device.

This is a really, really, good idea.

Do you lock the front door of your home before you go to sleep at night? Of course you do. It is a basic, obvious, and important thing to do to prevent unwanted intruders. Is it a 100% guarantee that a thief wont steal your stemware? Of course not. But locking the front door is a smart, basic practice because to *not* do it is like inviting in the bad guys.

Figure 2: System Password Required for Access

What's the Problem?

Physical access to a mobile phone, mobile device, or laptop is the easiest way to remove its contents. As a practical matter, you have to trust the people around you every day, otherwise you will either lose your mind, or you work in a prison. The point is, you could lose possession of your laptop, or mobile device, anytime.

According to Gartner, a technology research firm, a laptop is stolen every 53 seconds, which is about 600,000 per year. Imagine, for a moment, that your laptop was stolen. If it is secured with the password, then the simple act of opening your laptop and getting it to function is exponentially harder for the thief. If you are a billionaire, or a high-ranking politician, the thief may go through the trouble of sifting through your data. Otherwise, the thief who is most likely trying to make a buck off of the device, will not bother to try to get data off of the device. Data[iii] suggests that most stolen laptops are sold quickly; the thief simply wants to get the laptop out of their possession and won't bother trying to figure out your "front door" password.

> A laptop is stolen every 53 seconds, which is about 600,000 per year.

The fundamental problem is you can't be sure what happened to your data, and victims of stolen laptops find this element the most problematic. Did your family photos get republished on the Internet? Did someone read your emails? Did they find that file that contained all of your passwords? Did they reset the password on your Twitter account? By simply adding a password to the device, you can dramatically reduce the concern about the data.

But, your laptop does not actually have to be stolen for you to be exposed. Have you ever stepped away from your laptop at a coffee shop for a few seconds, or leave your laptop running at your desk for a few minutes? Did you know that someone can steal most or all of your system passwords from your computer with only a few seconds of physical access, if there is no system password set?

When you enter a username and password for a website for the first time, your browser (like Internet Explorer, Firefox, Safari, etc.) asks you if you want the browser to remember the password for you. **If you click 'yes,' then the browser stores the password.**

What you may not know is this password is STORED and VISIBLE, right on your computer.

Here's how to see where that password is stored; this is all the hacker or thief would need to do to steal your passwords given the opportunity of physical access to your computer for even a few seconds.

In Firefox (version 47.0), click the word "Firefox" in the toolbar, then select "preferences" in the drop-down menu. On the left-hand navigation bar, select "security." Then, on the right you will see a button called "Saved Logins." Then, click the "Show passwords" button. Then, you will see the username and password that you have chosen to store in Firefox. Its All Right There.

Rest assured, thieves know exactly how to do this. In other words, if a thief or hacker gets physical control of your laptop for even for few seconds, they can get your usernames and passwords to multiple accounts.

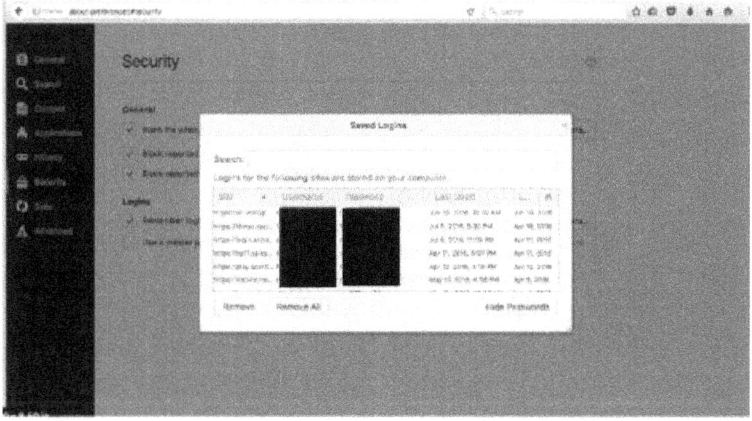

Figure 3: Screenshot of Firefox Security Window Exposing Passwords

Yes, this is a real screenshot. The real data is blocked with the black rectangles so you cannot see it, but all the information is right there just 5 clicks away from your homescreen.

And, you can do it on **Internet Explorer**, also:

Click to open User Accounts, then on the left pane, click "Manage your credentials." Click the vault that contains the username / password that you want to manage. You can see and edit the password from that screen.

Here is how to do the same thing on **Safari**:

In the toolbar of Safari, click preferences. In the window that appears, click the "passwords" icon and the top row. At the bottom of that window, click the checkbox next to "show passwords for selected sites."

Note: Safari does offer one other layer of protection because it will ask you for a password, but ***only*** if you use a password when you start up your computer. That way, somebody with temporary access to your computer cannot easily see your passwords if they are in Safari. Firefox ***does not*** have that layer of security.

Keep in mind that different products are doing different things when you activate the system password. While some systems are simply blocking a user from doing anything on the device without entering the password, other systems are actually using the password to encrypt the entire system, *and* all the data stored in the system. The iPhone is a great example of this:

iPhone Password

iPhone security is rather extraordinary, if you use a passcode. Here is how it works. When an iPhone is manufactured in the factory, there is a Secret encrypted key, which is exactly like a user identifier, which is unique to that phone, and burned into the hardware.

This key is literally created once, and can never be read by any program, ever. There is literally no way to get the key, and every iPhone has one. It is called the "secure enclave." The only thing that the iPhone, or any program running on the iPhone can ever possibly do is to give the secure enclave a task to do. Then, the secure enclave will give you the results of that task, *but it will never reveal the key*. If you set your iPhone to only open if you enter a passcode, then, according to Apple, the iPhone will "tangle" your passcode with the secure enclave, making your passcode part of the secret key. Apple has no way of knowing the secret key after you create a passcode, and the rest of the iPhone also does not know the key. That puts the power of unlocking the key exclusively in the hands of the person who set the passcode.

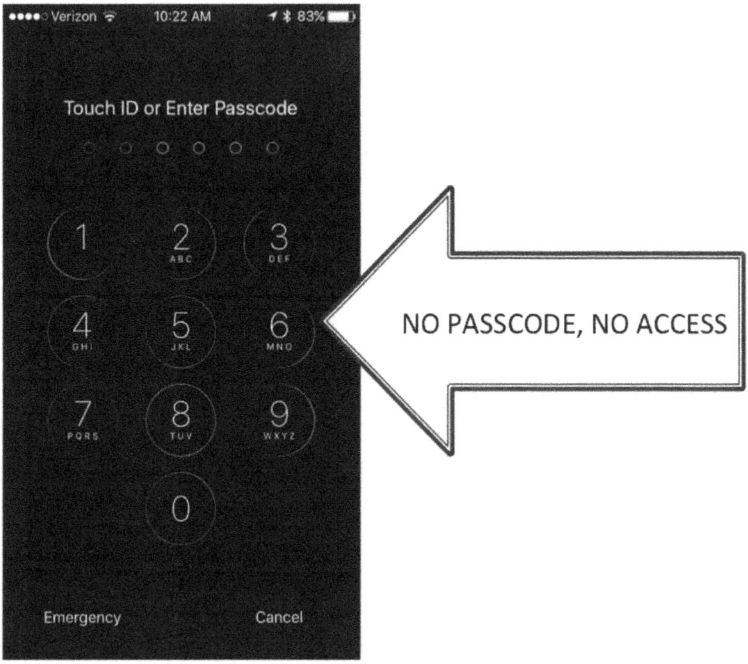

Figure 4: Example of iPhone Passcode Screen

It gets even better. Now that the passcode is set, literally everything on the iPhone is encrypted with this secret key. All of your emails, text messages, information in any of your apps, simply cannot be used without the passcode. In fact, if a technician physically opened a locked iPhone, physically removed the memory chip, and tried to read the information in that chip, that information would be hopelessly encrypted. What does hopelessly encrypted mean? It typically refers to an encryption method called AES 256 Kb, which essentially is a string of 256 ones and zeros. How long would it take to decrypt a string of 256 ones and zeros if you do not know the correct order? A strong computer can do about 2 billion calculations in a second. Imagine you could somehow connect 1 billion of these computers together working on the same problem at the same time. If such a computer could be built, it would still take that computer approximately seven times longer than the length of time that the universe has existed (the universe has been around for about 14 billion years) and it would require the power consumption of 150 nuclear power plants. Unless you have that kind of time, money, and access to a couple of hundred nuclear power plants, the data is **hopelessly encrypted** without the passcode. Cool, right?

This security is so extraordinary that literally the combined code-breaking ability of the US government failed to gain access to an iPhone because a passcode was used on the lock screen. No Kidding; the best of the best of the US government tried and failed.

The following story not only is a great example of how powerful this security technology is, but it also indicates that technology companies (like Apple) are trying to remove themselves from the ability to open the products that they manufacture if there customer uses the passcode. In other words, Apple literally does not want to be able to access a phone that it designs, manufactures, and sells if a user assigns a passcode to that phone. This is could be the start of a new chapter in technology, for you, the user of the device, are the only person that can gain access. All this through a simple passcode.

Apple vs. the FBI

It started with a murderous act that ended with 14 people dead and 22 seriously injured[iv]. The murderer [name withheld out of respect for the victims] was an employee of the San Bernardino County Department of Public Health who decided to murder his coworkers at a training event and Christmas party on December 2, 2015. The murderer and his co-conspirator were killed in the shootout with police hours later. The FBI opened an investigation the next day. Naturally, the FBI sought to collect all relevant evidence to the crime, and one of those pieces of evidence was the iPhone 5c that was issued to the murderer by his employer. But, the murderer protected his phone with a passcode. Without the passcode, the phone was hopelessly encrypted, so the FBI had to figure out the passcode.

The iPhone has a maximum of six letter and number combinations allowed for its passcodes. The straightforward method to crack the password is to try every possible combination, like this:

> Enter 000000. If that doesn't work, try;
> 000001. If that doesn't work, try;
> 000002. If that doesn't work, try;
>
> Later...
>
> Enter 999998. If that doesn't work, try;
> 999999. If that doesn't work, try;
> 99999a. If that doesn't work, try;
> 99999b. If that doesn't work, try;
>
> And later...

> Enter zzzzzx. If that doesn't work, try;
> zzzzzy. If that doesn't work, try;
> zzzzzz. That code must work because the two TRILLION (2,176,782,336 to be exact) other combination of letters and numbers were previously been tried.

This method is called "brute force", because it is neither clever nor subtle. It's one of the easiest software programs to write (this cannot be done manually; it would take hundreds of years.) In the case of an iPhone, it takes about 80 milliseconds for the iPhone to check whether or not a passcode is correct or not. That means the iPhone is capable of checking approximately 12.5 passwords per second assuming a passcode could be entered almost instantaneously by another computer. So, if the FBI had to check all possible combinations for this six-digit passcode before it could unlock the phone, it would take a maximum of five years! Clearly, an unreasonably long time to wait during a criminal investigation.

> **Back up your iPhone before testing the 10 passcode attempt limit or you will own an expensive paperweight.**

In addition to this method of taking an unreasonable amount of time, there was another serious problem. Apple had programmed a limit of 10 passcode attempts before it erased all data in the phone. In other words, if a user tries and fails to enter the passcode 10 times in a row into an iPhone, all of the data is lost forever. The iPhone will literally erase the passcode, which was used to create the secret, hopelessly unbreakable key that has encrypted all of the data stored on the phone. So, even if the FBI tried to get the data off the phone by some other sophisticated means, the data would never be able to be read.

> **NOTE**: If you are tempted to try to enter the wrong passcode into your iPhone ten times to see this work for yourself, all of your data will be lost unless you back up your phone first. If you do this without backing up your phone, then your iPhone becomes a very expensive paperweight.

But, the FBI, with all of its technical skills and expertise in security and cracking codes, was unable to turn "off" Apple's 10-attempt limit. So, the FBI turned to the only department in the US government that is actually better at cracking codes than the FBI: the National Security Agency, or NSA. But, the NSA could neither access the data nor remove the 10-attempt limit.

Just sit with that for moment.

The NSA, arguably the best code-cracking agency on earth, could not defeat the encryption that was built into the Apple iPhone. This is powerful stuff.

There was no one left to ask for help, except for Apple. In the past, Apple had complied with subpoenas ordering it to unlock Apple-made products that were owned by known criminals. And, Apple clearly built-in the ability to unlock its own phones in earlier versions of the iPhone. But, the phone involved with the San Bernardino murders was in the iPhone 5-series, which added the new level of encryption to which Apple intentionally designed to be unable to open if a passcode was added.

When the FBI thought is had assembled a reasonable, and legally valid argument, they went to Apple with a strong case, and a simple request: "remove the 10 attempt limit so we can attempt a brute force attack, and get access to the data to an iPhone that was used by a murderer in the months leading up to this terrible crime. " And, to make the FBI case stronger, the iPhone in question was issued to the murderer by his employer, and was therefore the property of the San Bernardino County Department of Public Health, which naturally had given consent for the phone to be opened by whatever means necessary.

But, Apple refused the FBI's request. Here's exactly what Apple's CEO, Tim Cook, said in a press statement at the time:

> "We have great respect for the professionals at the FBI, and we believe their intentions are good. Up to this point, we have done everything that is both within our power and within the law to help them. But now the U.S. government has asked us for something we simply do not have, and something we consider too dangerous to create. They have

asked us to build a backdoor to the iPhone."
Tim Cook, CEO, Apple Computers [v]

So, the FBI went to a US Federal Judge. Interestingly, they did not seek a subpoena instead they believed that

Figure 5: Cartoon Depicting the Danger of Forcing Apple to create a 'Back Door' to the iPhone.

a 225 year-old US law was all they needed to compel Apple to create a process by which it could defeat the measures that it designed into the iPhone.

The Judge in the case, Sherri Pym, issued a court order, mandating Apple to comply based on the All Writs Act of ***1789***.

You read that correctly; a law written in 1789 was cited to compel Apple to create software to defeat some of most advanced cryptography ever created. No Kidding.

What is the All Writs Act of 1789? It basically gives law enforcement authority to compel private companies to help carry out search warrants.

This may have been one of the most important moments of United States privacy rights since the 1960s, and it all happened in February 2016. The government wanted to use this case as justification to make any company unlock any device it manufactured, or at least create the software and processes necessary to unlock any device it manufactures without having to get a subpoena - *just a search warrant.*

Remember, we're still just talking about the passcode to unlock an iPhone, a technology design by Apple that is so secure that the FBI and the NSA combined could not break.

In the end, Apple prevailed by default. The FBI purchased a method to unlock the phone of the San Bernardino murderer from a private security company, and subsequently dropped the case against Apple. Understandably, many are curious about this private company, and how it was able to defeat Apple's security. Apple is curious about that, too, but as of the writing of this book, we have not resolved the problem.

From a privacy standpoint, this issue is something to watch as it develops. Lawmakers and legislators are now attempting to pass laws[vi] that would permanently accomplish what the FBI could not.

Habit

If you use a laptop, or a mobile device, or both, use the password option to unlock the device to prevent unauthorized access.

It's a simple habit, it will give you peace of mind that someone with momentary access to your device can't see all of your passwords that you have stored in your browser, or have access to anything else. And, worst-case, if someone steals your laptop or mobile device, you can rest more comfortably knowing that they will not be able to get to your personal information, private data, names of your friends in your contact list, and private passwords to online accounts.

If you are not sure how to set a password, go to google.com and search the following phrase for Mobile devices:

How to enable a password on [NAME OF YOUR DEVICE, EX: Samsung S5; iPhone 6s] ***lock screen***

... and Google this phrase for laptops and desktops:

How to enable a screensaver password for [NAME OF OPERATING SYSTEM EX: Windows, OSx El Capitan, etc.]

Get into the habit of using this password/passcode every time you turn on your device, or wake up your device from sleep mode or screen saver mode. You will be glad you did.

Digital Habit 2:

SHUT THE BACK DOOR, TOO!

Email access represents one of the most common forms of hacking. Think about it, if a hacker wants to get access to your email, not only can they read all of your mail, but the hacker can also reset the password of any account attached to that email address by clicking "Reset my password." If that happens, the hacker can reset your password to whatever new password they like, and they can do that to any account that uses that email address. And that's just one example of what the hacker can do.

As we discussed in the previous section, security experts will tell you to make every password on every account at least as long as the Nile River, never write your password anywhere, and change all your passwords eight times a week, etc.

Here's the point. **If you only have time to really protect one of your passwords, it should be the password to your email account**. Ironically, your email password is probably one of the only passwords that nobody asks you to reset or maintain on a regular basis. So, if you're like most people, the password that is letting you read your email right now is the same password that you have been using for a year? Three years? Ten years? This is the riskiest thing you can do online.

> The riskiest thing you can do online is not to protect the password of your primary email account.

While this point could probably be made without a movie reference, what's the fun in that?

Have you ever seen any of the Lord of the Rings movies, or read any of the books? The basic premise was that the evil Sauron created nine rings that provided power to those who carried them. But, Sauron also created the 10th ring that ruled the other nine. ***Your email is the 10th ring.*** While passwords are designed to protect your accounts on multiple systems, they all have one thing in common: **your email**.

How They Do It

Hackers and thieves use a variety of methods to try to gain access to your email. For example, they use a "Dictionary" attack on you (and thousands of other accounts) just to see if they can find a simple word in the dictionary, or another common password. And, yes, they know that the letter "o" can be substituted with a zero, and a letter "i" can se substituted with the number "1."

Or, maybe the thief purchased your password on the deep web because it was stolen from another site, and you happen to use the password that was stolen as the password on your email. ***See Digital Habit #5 (Embrace Amnesia)*** for more on these forms of attack.

Why They Do It

As discussed in the Introduction, remember to remove reason and logic when you look for the motivation of a hacker, but the motivation of the thief is much more direct. They want money. But as a practical matter, how can a thief monetize your email if they get the password? Many, many different ways.

Like most things, if a thief can steal it, the thief can find someone to buy it.

Usernames and passwords are available for sale on the Internet, generally on the Deep Web, not the Surface Web (see 'Definitions' section at the end of this book). Depending on the website, the price for each username and password can vary. And, in the case where the thief already has your email address, and the password to your email, they simply run a program that tests whether or not they can reset your password on some of the more popular sites by simply activating the, "I forgot my password" link, which practically every website uses. Or, perhaps you made it easy on the thief by using the same username and password on your Facebook account, your Wal-Mart account, your FedEx account, and your Twitter account. The thieves' software tool will try all popular sites first just to see what works.

After your password is successfully reset, the thief covers their tracks by deleting the emails that were necessary to reset your password. Passwords on different accounts sell for different cash values. For example, a notable cyber security expert, Brian Krebs[vii], wrote this sample of the price people are willing to pay for passwords:

> *One prominent credential seller in the underground peddles iTunes accounts for $8, and Fedex.com, Continental.com and United.com accounts for USD $6. Groupon.com accounts fetch $5, while $4 buys hacked credentials at registrar and hosting provider Godaddy.com, as well as wireless providers Att.com, Sprint.com, Verizonwireless.com, and Tmobile.com. Active accounts at Facebook and Twitter retail for just $2.50 apiece.*
>
> *Some crime shops go even lower with their prices for hacked accounts, charging between $1 to $3 for active accounts at dell.com, overstock.com, walmart.com, tesco.com,*

bestbuy.com and target.com, to name just a few.

Source: http://krebsonsecurity.com/2013/06/the-value-of-a-hacked-email-account/

But, again, sometimes the hacker is not a thief that wants your money, or wants to sell your password for money. They just want to cause damage. One of the most damaging, non-financial hacks of all time is that of Mat Honan.

Crushingly Hacked

Mat was, in his own words, "crushingly hacked' in 2012[viii]. At the time, Mat was a senior writer for Wired magazine, and a hacker targeted him personally. The hacker seemed to want to embarrass Mat by accessing Mat's Twitter account, and posting content that Mat would have never posted himself. But, in an effort to cause as much damage as possible, the hacker destroyed all of the data in Mat's laptop, and mobile devices, including more than a year's worth of photos. At the time, Mat had a one-year-old daughter, which means that he lost every photo he had ever taken of his daughter in her entire life. Mat lost many other things of value, including documents and e-mails that were not backed up, but the loss of every photo of the lifespan of his 1-year-old must have been devastating. But none of the items Mat lost likely had any cash value at all; the hacker must have had another reason. Again, remove logic and accountably before you try to understand why someone would do this.

The point is, the attack on Mat Honan began by the hacker taking over his Gmail account. Once the hacker had access to Gmail, the hacker went to Twitter, and changed Mat's password on his Twitter account using the "I forgot my password" function. Twitter sent an email to Mat's Gmail account with a link to reset the password, which the hacker used to change his Twitter password. The hacker could have simply deleted the emails from Twitter to cover their tracks, but instead, deleted the entire Google account.

With Mat's Twitter account successfully compromised by the hacker, the hacker began to broadcast terrible messages of racism and homophobia under Mats Twitter handle. But the hacker wasn't done yet; the next target was Mat's AppleID the hacker broke into and used it to remotely erase all of the data on his iPhone, iPad, and MacBook, including the photos of his daughter.

A hacker this determined, and this skilled, is likely going to cause a lot of damage if they take the time to target an individual. But, the basic point of the story is that the whole attack started by getting the password to Mats email.

Habits

Most articles written on the subject of password protection are extreme, and are intended to apply every rule to all of your dozens of online accounts. If you're not going to take the time to protect all of your accounts, at least take the time to protect this one account: your primary email account. There are actually two basic habits that can help here:

A) Two factor authentication. If you use a Gmail account, or any mail client that you access through a browser, then you may be able to turn 'on' two factor authentication. This means that when you log into your account, you will receive a text message to your smart phone, and you will need to enter that text message into a special field that comes up on the screen. So, if a hacker, or thief, manages to acquire your password to your primary email account, they would also have to have access to your mobile phone, which is exponentially harder to do. After you log in to your online account, go to the 'Help' screen and search the term, 'Security' or 'Two-Factor Authentication.' If your search yields a result, then follow the instructions to turn it 'on.' If not, your account probably does not provide this feature.

B) Create a reminder: if you are not reminded to change the password on your email account, then make a calendar event for yourself as often as you tolerate. At a minimum, use the beginning and end of daylight savings time to ensure that you change it twice per year, or change your email password whenever you change the batteries in your smoke detectors.

C) For tips on how to create good passwords, and why you should do that, see Digital Habit #5: Embrace Insomnia.

Digital Habit #3:

Why-Fi

Why do you use WiFi?

Well, if you are connecting to the Internet through a laptop, WiFi is the best, and least expensive way to connect. If you use a mobile device that has a cellular data plan, then connecting to WiFi is far less expensive method of connecting to the Internet compared to using your cellular data.

So, if you are like most people, you're happy when your computer automatically connects to a Wi-Fi network when you are not at home, or at work because it saves you money. You sit down at a coffee shop, you flip open your laptop, open your browser, and find that you are already connected to the Internet. "Excellent!" you say. What could be bad about that? Free Internet access, and you don't use your expensive cellular data. Best of all, there is no password to remember. Perfect, right?

Wrong.

Why? The answer is simple: **the owner of a Wi-Fi network can see everything you do through your connected device.** Every site you visit, every keystroke you enter, everything is visible to the Wi-Fi network owner.

If that is news to you, then you are probably thinking that the remedy is simple: just don't connect to networks that you don't know, right? Well, there is a problem there too.

Hackers and thieves are clever. They create free, easy to join Wi-Fi networks with common names (myWiFi, FreeWiFi, Lobby, Guest, etc.) because you may have visited a Wi-Fi network with the same name in the past. After you join a Wi-Fi network once, your device will trust a network with the same name (unless you disable that feature). The problem is, the network is only identified by its name. (The "name" of a Wi-Fi network is a “Service Set Identifier,” or simply ‘SSID’). **So, if two Wi-Fi networks have the exact same name, or SSID, your laptop cannot tell them apart.** All the thief needs to do is create a Wi-Fi network that has the exact same name of the other popular networks to gain a legion of computers to trust it.

For example, a popular home router is made by Cisco under the brand-name “Linksys.” Many of these Wi-Fi routers were programmed with a default SSID of “linksys.” As a result, there were tens of thousands of

Wi-Fi networks set up by simply plugging in the device, creating Wi-Fi networks called "linksys". If you have ever joined a network by that name, then your computer will assume that ANY network by the same name must be a trusted network. So, the work of the thief is pretty easy; just set up a malicious Wi-Fi network with the name "Linksys" and many (if not most) devices will automatically trust that network.

Once connected, the malicious "Linksys" network can do whatever it likes to your computer.

And, if the stark simplicity of this attack is not surprising enough, here's one more layer: some Wi-Fi routers ship with both a default SSID, *and* a default username and password! Unfortunately, many people do not change the default SSID, username, or password when they purchase and install a new Wi-Fi system.

CONSUMER TIP

Always change the default username and password on any electronic equipment you buy. If you ever see a prompt that says, "update default", Click the yes button!!.

This makes for easy work on the part of the thieves. All they need to do is look up the default username password, and see if it works on a given system. If the default username and password allows a thief to login, then... nothing good happens to anyone who uses that Wi-Fi connection. The hacker can bring that system under his or her complete control, including all of the computers and devices that connect to it. And if you thought it might be hard for hackers to keep a database of the default usernames and passwords of different kinds of systems, well, there is a website for that. The website that keeps track of default usernames and passwords by system is called: www.routerpasswords.com

Generally, these attacks are called "Man in the Middle" attacks. But, that name is not descriptive enough. A more accurate name is "Thief in the Middle", because nobody would go to the trouble of setting up a malicious, and cloaked, Wi-Fi network for noble, or non-profitable, purposes.

Believe it or not, it gets worse. The hackers that use the SSID, or exploit the default username and password on the Wi-Fi network, are far less dangerous than some others in the hacker community. Here is how the more sophisticated hackers use Wi-Fi to trick you into joining their network. They build fake websites to lure you into giving over your information.

For example, the thief can replicate popular websites that look like the real thing, but are instead swarming with malware that will be installed on your computer. See example on the next page:

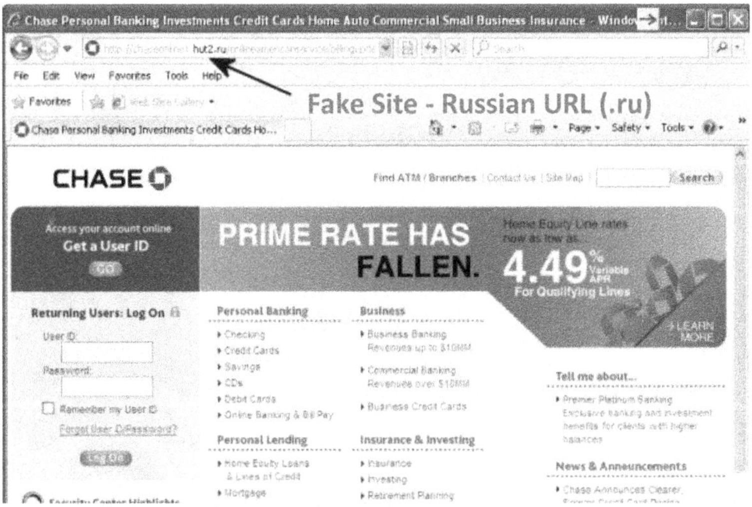

Figure 6: Fake, or "Spoofed" Bank Web Page

The grand prize is your username and password to a financial account, or your credit card number.

If you are on Wi-Fi and you entered www.chase.com, but the website looks unusual, like a Russian URL (see Figure 6, above), you need to close the page. While you think you are logging in to your site, the thief is capturing your username and password, and will be able to take over your session at any time -- all seemingly with your permission!

Habits

The only way to protect yourself from a Thief -in-the-Middle attack is to not join the compromised Wi-Fi network. But, you can't rely on the websites you see while using an infected Wi-Fi network because the attacker will usually let you pass through the malicious network to the website you wanted so you don't suspect anything is wrong. Every website you visit will appear to function normally, until the attacker sees you try to access a website that they have spoofed, or until they get you to download the malicious software. Then, you may see a problem,

When you power-on your computer, take a moment to check the name of your Wi-Fi network. At the top or bottom of your computer screen, look for the Wi-Fi icon on the right of this page, and simply click it to see the name of the network to which you are connected. If you don't recognize it, or you did not mean to connect to that network, find the "forget this network" button and click it so you don't automatically connect to that network again.

Figure 7: WiFi Icon

And, you can set your computer to never remember a Wi-Fi network that you join; just go to google.com and search the term:

"***How do I set my*** [Name of computer, like MacBook or Samsung 6S] ***to forget all wifi networks***"

Make sure you manually click "remember this network" only for networks that you trust, like at home or your office.

Also, check your network connection whenever you log in to a financial network, such as online connections to your bank or credit union. Make sure you are on a trusted network in a trusted location before you log in.

As an added precaution, never log into your financial accounts when you are on a shared or public Wi-Fi system like a coffee shop, library, or other public area.

This is one of the more difficult attacks to defeat, but it is worth it to modify your habits for this one. Remember, it takes about three seconds to check the name of your Wi-Fi connection, and it is an easy way to avoid an attack.

Digital Habit 4:

PHISHERMEN LIE

You get emails that promote lots of things, offer lots of things, and sometimes plea for help. They are all different versions of spam and phishing emails. Although there are many forms of this attack, the most common, by far, are emails with either the name of a website link that you are asked to click, or an attachment that you are asked to open. The content of the message will say anything, however outrageous or benign, just to get you to either click the link or open the attachment.

Here is a disturbing real-life example that happened in 2015. A colleague (we'll call her Betty) received a text message from a friend she had known most of her life (we'll call him Larry) that read, "I've got about half of the money together now and will wire it as soon as I get to the bank. Can you wait until tomorrow for the rest of it?"

The problem was, Betty never asked for money. A thief used malware that had infected Betty's computer to send messages to specific people in Betty's contact list without her knowledge. So, Larry got a message that seemed to be from Betty that said:

> *Larry you have to help me. Took a trip to Ghana, got mugged near hotel. Need $10,000 to get home. At Bank of Ghana now; please wire funds - wiring instructions attached. Very scared, please help!*

Naturally Larry was alarmed, so he wrote a reply email that said:

> *Hang in there; running to broker's office to liquidate, then to bank to wire the funds.*

But, the thief had control of Betty's email, so the thief was able to reply to Larry:

> *Thank you so much!*

Thinking he had verified the message, Larry went to get the funds for Betty.

But then, Larry got lucky. He had stepped away from his computer to walk to his car so he could wire the money from his bank. But, by stepping away from his computer, Larry was forced to use his text message (not email) to give a status update while he was walking across the parking lot. By communicating with Betty via text message, and not via email which is how he received the original plea for help, there was a second mode of communication (text, not email) used, and of course, the thief did not have access to read or block messages from Betty's text message account. Betty called Larry, and the attack was revealed.

> Socially engineered Trojans (emails with a link or an attachment) are responsible for hundreds of millions of successful hacks each year. Against those numbers, all other hacking types are just noise." Info World Magazine.

To prevent this from happening to you is an easy fix; never trust an email that is requesting that you act in any way (Click this link, open this attachment, wire me money because I'm drowning in a swamp in Ghana). But, if you want to respond because perhaps you have a group of friends that recently set out to go swamp hiking in Ghana, *you must initiate the response through a different mode of communication.*

For example, if you receive an email that seems to be from your bank, demanding an immediate response from you for some reason, just open your browser, (a different mode of communication than email) manually enter your bank's web site address, and log into your online banking account. If the notification was legitimate, then you will find it when you login. If that doesn't work, pick up the phone and call your bank. Do <u>anything</u> but respond directly through the email that contained the Notification.

As for the swamp hikers in Ghana who wrote the email pleading with you to wire money to them, like Larry, obviously never wire money to a friend in need without speaking to them directly.

Like most attacks, the attacker, hacker or thief needs your permission for the most damaging attacks. You have to agree to open the email, or click the link, or wire the money, or answer the phone.

Permission

During your lifetime, you will probably receive a phone call, at home or at work, when the voice at the other and says, "Hi, this is Steve from tech support. Is your system operating a little slow today?" Tell him you need to call him back, and ask his extension and direct dial number. You will either hear, “No Problem call extension 25 and ask for Steve”, or you will simply hear the “click" sound of the caller hanging up on you, because they were a hacker and they were caught.

Of course your system is operating a little slow today; when are we not frustrated if a web site even takes a few seconds to load. This is an easy kind of phone scam where the caller tries to get your permission to download software directly into your computer. After that, the software that is loaded onto your computer- which is almost always guaranteed to be malicious - will be able to do almost anything the attacker wants your computer to do, including, divulging your secrets, your content, you're computing power, anything at all.

Again, the good news is that hackers and thieves need permission to install malicious software on your computer. Makers of software over the years have intentionally made it difficult to install malicious software without you granting some form of permission, or executing a file, or some action from you, like clicking a link, or opening an attachment. Here is a garden-variety example of a hacker that just wants the recipient to click the attachment.

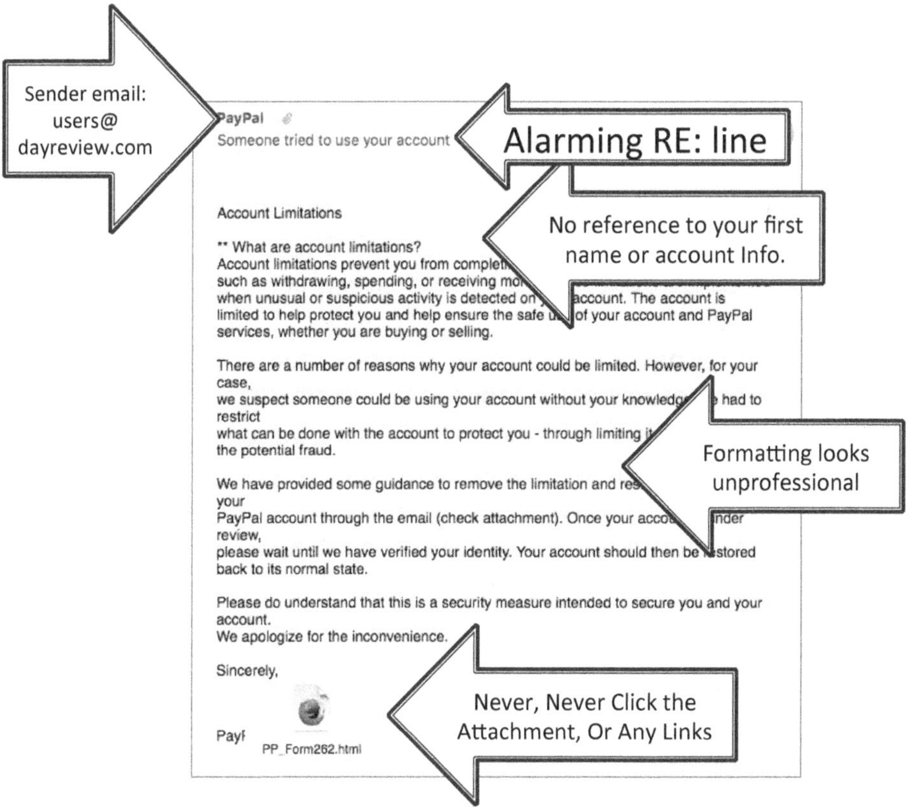

Figure 8: Malicious Email Sample

In the email on the previous page, there are several clues that indicate this is a hacker. And, even if none of these clues were in the email, your habit should be to never click the attachment because there are sophisticated hackers that know how to make their emails look legitimate; this "phisherman" simply didn't take the time to bait his hook better. In case you're wondering why anyone would even bother if nobody would click on such an obvious scam email, because some people do. It's just the law of large numbers. If this hacker has a few million email addresses, and only 1 in 1,000 recipients actually open this attachment, that is still thousands of computers infected by the hackers virus without a high degree of effort by the hacker.

The attachment in this example was particularly nasty; it was a Trojan that included two different programs designed to find the victim's personal information, including login credentials to bank accounts, plus another program designed to look for credit card numbers stored on the computer, and finally some good old-fashioned spyware to keep tabs on what the victim is doing on their computer. On the day that email was received, the thief who sent it probably infected a few thousand computers with those programs. And that was just one attack from one hacker.

Let's assume, for a moment, that this email was a bit more convincing; checking it's legitimacy is easy:

Start with the email address. If the actual email address is not readily displayed, just click the name (In the case of this example, click the word "PayPal" In the "From" line in the header of the email - Again, NEVER click anything in the body of email.) In this case, the email address did not seem to indicate that the sender was actually an employee, or representative, of PayPal. The sender's email address was,"users@dayreview.com."

Every other element of the example of the spam email simply makes it easier to determine if you need to take the time to check the email, or if it is so obviously spam that you should add it to your junk mail.

Of course, legitimate businesses need permission, too. Consumers can be unsettled to know how many different computer networks are aware of who you are and what you are doing at any moment in time and this does not even count the other networks that track your activity every time you go on to the Internet, or log into a computer.

Privacy policies are becoming more prevalent with companies, at least in the United States and the EU. In fact, sweeping new privacy laws[ix], may soon be requiring legitimate companies to establish new and more efficient practices not just for your financial data, but for your personal data as well. Every legitimate database that tracks you as a consumer today needs to receive your permission to do that. For example, if you choose a loyalty program from your bank or credit accounts, review the sign-up screens carefully and make sure that you are selecting or deselecting the permission that they will ask you for regarding their ability to track and use your personal information.

The offers that will come to you over the next few years will be increasingly common as the payment industry and loyalty industries grapple with new models that center around mobile devices. For example: a retail cashier may offer you a big discount on the purchase you are about to make if you "just tap your phone right here," as he points to the reader on his cash register. If you do that, rest assured that somewhere, on some computer, on some faraway network, a new account was opened just for you and that account will look for as much information about your shopping patterns and behaviors as possible.

The other side of the privacy issue is that you can actually get better discounts for things that you want if you are willing to trade some of your privacy. For example, have you ever received those blue oversized coupons that are sent out routinely by Bed Bath and Beyond? Did you notice that after you used every one of the $10-off coupons that they sent to your home, the amount eventually changed to $20-off. Why did they do that? Because they noticed that when you use a coupon, the average amount of your transaction quadruples. They look at the profit each time the dollar value of your transaction went up, and wondered if you would spend more money still if they doubled your coupon amount from $10 to $20. So they tested that theory by sending you a $20-off coupon, and then looked at the amount of your transaction when you used it. If they liked the result, then you keep receiving the $20-off coupon periodically; If not, you start receiving the $10 coupon again.

The point is, if you do not want to be in Bed Bath and Beyond's database, don't use their coupons. If you do not want your local grocery store to know anything about you, do not join their club program, but you will likely give up the benefit of some sale prices (which require you to use their club card to get the discount) plus the benefit of using the points you accumulate to purchase whatever you can through their catalogs.

So, it really is a cost versus-benefit-decision. If you don't use a coupon, you don't get the discount but you also don't get tracked on their network database. If you don't sign up for club card, again you lose the discounts and benefits, but you avoid getting added to another network database.

If you were not aware of these issues as you signed up for all of these various programs over the years, don't worry. The next decade will give you a chance to start over on all of them. If you are offered a program that does not seem to give you enough privacy options, then simply do not join it.

There will be other programs that will give you access to the same discounts with better privacy; you just have to find them. Also, you may need to have a little patience. The best programs with the most privacy flexibility and the highest level of rewards may take some time to materialize. Most of these legitimate programs will be based on your email, giving yet another source of incoming emails. Separating the legitimate offers from the illegitimate ones will seem like a hard thing to do. But, it is actually simple and straightforward. What follows are two legitimate emails that allow you to see clear difference when compared to the hacker email displayed earlier:

Figure 9: Legitimate email from Web Merchant

Notice how the email address (freepeople@freepeople.com) appears to be from the actual company. But, as professional as this looks, it is still just an image with some text, which any hacker could replicate. So, don't click any links or open any attachments.

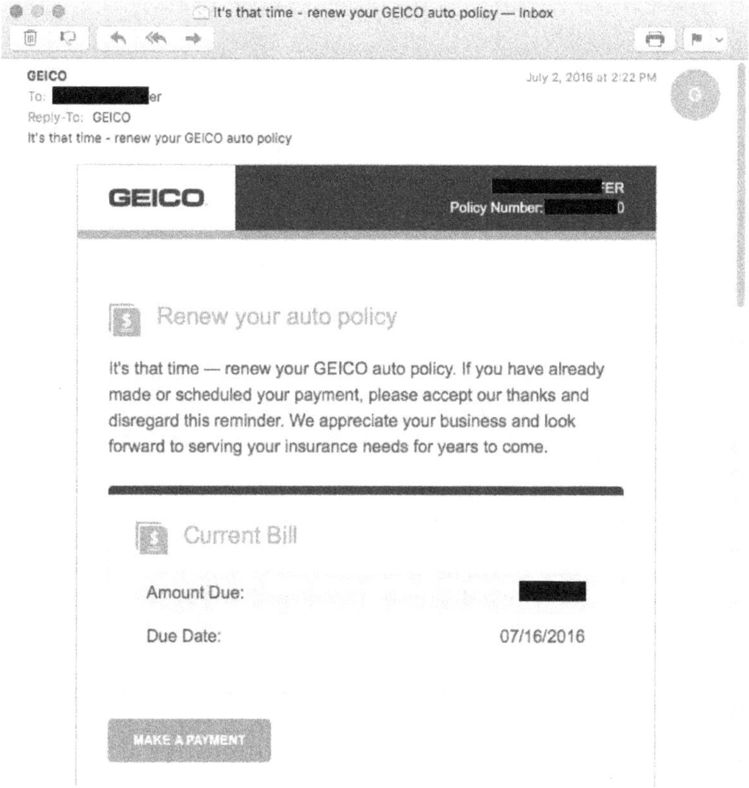

Figure 10: Legitimate Email from Insurance Company

Notice how this message is much more specific. It refers to the user by name, lists the user account number and account balance, and other specific information about the user account. But, a good hacker could fake this, too, so don't click any links.

Habits

When you receive an email with either a link to a website, or an attachment, here is what to do:

First, look at the email address of the sender, then, simply do one of three things: junk it, verify it without email (if possible), or manually open the website.

Junk It

If the sender is not somebody you know, or from a company you have never heard of, and there is anything that strikes you suspicious about the message, click the "junk" button in your email to add it to your junk list. You're done; you don't have to think about this message again.

Verify (without using your email)

On the other hand, if you think the sender's email may be legitimate, then take a moment to verify that the sender meant to send the message. Obviously, apply your common sense filter, and try to remember if the sender just told you in a phone call that he was sending you a document in an email attachment, or if you just did a password reset request from EBay, and Ebay sent you an email with a link 10 seconds later.

Otherwise, take a few seconds to verify that the sender meant to send you an email with a link, or an attachment.

Here is the catch; **try not to verify an email by sending another email.** Try to use some other form of communication -- the easiest is text messaging.

For example, if you think Dan sent you an email that contains an attachment, and the sender's address in the email is an address that you know is Dan's correct email, you still cannot be 100% sure that Dan actually meant to send the message.

Why?

Keep in mind that Dan's computer may be infected with a virus that is capable of sending email addresses to everyone in Dan's contact list without Dan knowing. Remember Larry and Betty? An infected computer could be sending you a message that appears to be from Dan. It is rare, but an infected computer could also be programmed to automatically respond, "all good" to anybody that replies to the malicious email.

That is why you want to try to avoid using email to verify the email. This doesn't mean you need to open an FBI investigation, instead, just send a quick text message like this:

> *"got email from your address. said to click link to cnn article. From U?"*

Just 14 words, and a few seconds to write. Or, if you and Dan communicate often with Skype chat, FaceTime, AOL messenger, or anything else, use that. Or, just pick up the phone and speak to Dan. The point is that you're not using the same channel through which you received the suspicious message.

If email is your only choice, use it if you have to. **But, be sure to create a new email (never forward the suspicious email to anyone),** and address your email to an address that you think is the real sender. In your email ask them if they sent you an email with an attachment/ link. Mention the time the email was sent, and the subject line, so the sender has an easier time checking their system. It only takes a few seconds, and it confirms if they are they sender. Here is a simple message:

> *"Hi Dan,*
>
> *I just received an email with an attachment from your email address. The RE: line was, "Open the attachment or time itself will end" and it was sent at 10:46 AM on July 7, 2016.*
>
> *Did you send it?"*

Again, never forward the message to Dan just in case it is malicious, because Dan could accidentally activate the virus on his computer. If that happens, Dan is probably going to drop you from his Christmas list.

Remember, if Dan replies "no," even though it came from his regular email address, remember *not* to add the suspicious email to your junk email because it will automatically send Dan's future emails to your junk folder. Instead move the suspicious email straight to your trashcan.

Again, assume that some of the things hackers do are just for fun, so if the hacker can't get you to infect your computer by opening the malicious attachment, then maybe they can disrupt a friendship by getting you to add a friend to your junk email (or spam) list.

Go Directly to the Website

In the example of spam email in this chapter, the email tries to appear to be an email from PayPal. Also in this chapter, are legitimate examples of emails from other companies, specifically Geico and Free People. But, one thing is true for all of them; you probably could not easily verify that they were really sent by the company. Who would you send the email to, and how long would you have to wait for a reply.

So, if you cannot verify the email by easily contacting the sender, how do you protect yourself. It's easy:

First, open your Internet browser (ex: Safari, Firefox, Explorer, or the like).

Then, manually type the URL for the home page of the site, like:

- www.FreePeople.com
- www.Geico.com
- www.Paypal.com
- ...or whatever site you think sent you an email.

If you are not sure about the web address for the home page, then use Google or Yahoo, or other search engine if you need to, ***but the point is that you are initiating the web page manually, and not by clicking the link in the email you received.*** Don't worry about the convenience that you are giving up, because the link in the email probably takes you to a page that is available right on the home page of the website to begin with.

Remember the legitimate email from the web merchant, Free People? Did you see that it contained a link to a sale item? It was, 50% off Flares.

Figure 11: Close-Up on Sale item in Web Merchant Email

You may think that the only way to get that sale price is to click the link, but it is usually not. This is what you see when you manually typed the web address to this merchant at the time this email was sent:

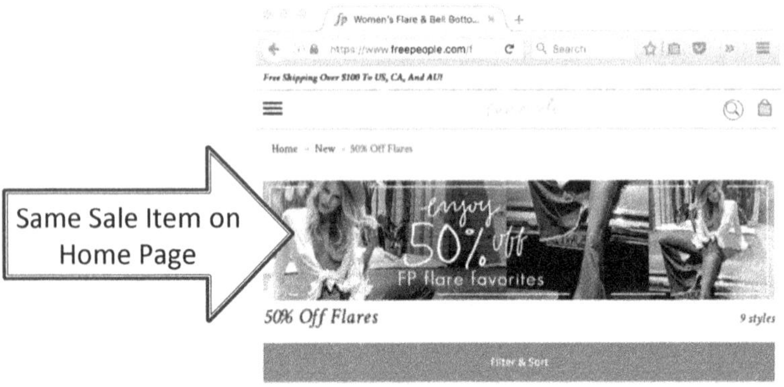

Figure 12: Web Merchant Home Page - Sale is Visible

There it is: 50% off Flares! And, if you did not immediately see what you were looking for, you could log in or do a simple search.

Bottom line, manually typing the name of the website into your browser will only take a few extra seconds and little effort to find what you are looking for, but it is a critical part of this habit and will help you avoid many kinds of attacks.

Digital Habit #5:

EMBRACE AMNESIA

So in Chapter 2 you read that if you only have time to protect one account, protect your primary email account. In this chapter, you will receive some ideas about password protection that may be easier to live with than your current system. Most people keep some sort of cheat-sheet for their passwords; a list either handwritten or electronic that helps you keep track of all of your passwords.

Spoiler alert: this chapter suggests that you throw your list away.

Primary Email

As a reminder, if you are only going to implement good password habits around one password, make it your primary email. Your other important emails like your bank account will likely force good habits on you. But, all of your other accounts deserve protection, too. Consider the possibility of using the habits suggested in this chapter for any account that you use regularly.

Passwords are fundamentally broken in a world where most of us have dozens or hundreds of passwords. There is no safe or efficient way to keep them all straight. Here you have to pick your poison, and there are a number of ways to manage: Fundamentally, you either remember the password, don't remember and write it down, or have a computer remember it for you.

Hackers and thieves know how much you hate passwords, and they know that you often have no choice but to take shortcuts around password security. Here are some common attacks:

Dictionary Attack

Let's assume that most people use a single word for their password. Logical assumption, because the term is password,' not 'passwordS' or passPHRASE.'

In a dictionary attack, the attacker starts with a long list of words, and variations of words. These lists can be used over and over again, and can also be bought and sold. So, over time, these dictionaries have become more and more comprehensive, constantly adding new words, and variations of words that may be used as passwords. A dictionary attack might try all the words in a dictionary, and simple variations of words, such as 's1mple,' or '3asy.' A dictionary attack also might include other commonly used passwords or combinations of letters and numbers like 'password1,' or 'h@cker.' Of course, at the top of the dictionary list are passwords that have been successfully stolen recently.

And, the attack takes less time than you might think. For example, Webster's dictionary has about 470,000 English words. Let's assume there are 100 variations and combinations of each word, such as:

- dictionary
- Dictionary
- dicti0nary
- D1ct1onary
- Dictiona3y
- dIcTiOnArY
- ...etc.

Also, multiply each by variation by 200 to account for the addition of a digit or two at the beginning or end of the word, such as:

- 11dictionary
- dictionary99

By this math, 100 variations x 200 extra digits = 20,000 combinations per word. So, if there are 470,000 words in the dictionary, and 20,000 possible combinations of each word, that's nine billion, four hundred-million (9,400,000,000) combinations.
The big question is: how many passwords can be checked in a second? Ten? One Hundred? A good workstation can try about 100 Million (100,000,000) per second[x], without getting too elaborate. A supercomputer using a well-designed array of graphics

cards or similarly high-speed processors can check about 1 billion per second.

But, let's keep our feet on the ground, and assume a reasonably sophisticated hacker can try about 100 million different passwords per second. So if a good dictionary attack needs to check about 9.4 billion combinations of usernames and passwords, that would take a good hacker about 90 seconds to try them all.

In other words, this is child's play.

Dictionary lists have become sophisticated enough to use some common combinations of words, like "MyCat" or "PrettyFlower." The use of these common phrases will vary from list to list, but given that not every word in the dictionary is necessarily part of a common phrase, a conservative estimate is that common phrases could triple the length of a list. Again, not a substantial difference for the time it takes to complete the attack; without the common phrases, the attack would take 90 seconds. With the common phrases, it would take 6 minutes. This is still not a substantial change.

Suppose you used two RANDOM words in your password, instead of one. It would have to be two completely disassociated words, such as "HappyCrutch" or "FlyBook." For a Dictionary attack to work, the list would have to be substantially longer.

How substantially? In round numbers, if a dictionary attack focused on single-word passwords and takes a reasonably sophisticated hacker about 90 seconds to complete, a dictionary attack focused on double-word passwords would take that same hacker about 28,000 years. The math is simple: 9.4 billion multiplied by 9.4 billion is 8,836,000,000,000,000,000. The number of combinations in a two-word dictionary attack is clearly ineffective.

This is why you want to choose a 'password' that is comprised of two random, unassociated words.

Of course, security experts know about dictionary attacks, and have taken measures to defeat these attacks within their computer networks. Obviously, most humans can not type 100 million passwords per second for the same username, so computer systems set alarms and other controls to defeat the attacker.

> A sophisticated hacker needs about 1.5 minutes to try every combination of a one - word passwords, but about 28,000 years to try every combination of two - word passwords.

The easiest way to defeat this type of attack is to simply slow down the number of attempts allowed per username in a second. Ever notice what happens when you accidentally enter the wrong password in your online banking site more than once? You may get a message such as, "you've entered the wrong username too many times. Please wait one minute and try again." Obviously, being allowed to make one attempt per minute will slow down the attacker that would prefer to make a few billion attempts per minute.

In addition, other sites will allow a finite number of total attempts before suspending the account. For example, a bank may allow a total of 10 attempts to enter their password correctly before freezing the account and instructing the user to "visit their local branch" to reactivate their account. That will enable the bank to see the person face-to-face, and ask for physical identification like a drivers license before reactivating the account.

Password Reuse

If a dictionary attack is so easy to defeat with basic enterprise security tactics, why would anyone bother? The answer: because not every enterprise uses basic enterprise security tactics. In other words, no hacker will try a Dictionary attack against Bank of America. A more likely target is a social media site, or a retail site, which is more interested in your convenience as a user then employing state-of-the-art security countermeasures to their enterprise systems. That's where the password– reuse problem comes in.

Hackers and thieves are constantly testing websites to see whether they employ the basic cyber security rules to protect their usernames and passwords, or not. When a hacker finds an insecure website, they go to work to collect as many valid username password combinations as possible. At 90 seconds per username, and infinite lists of usernames available on the Deep Web, it could take weeks of computer time, but the user could accumulate thousands of valid usernames and passwords from an unprotected site.

But, so what? Who wants to exploit the accounts of thousands of people who login every day to, for example, a site for people studying interesting birds or looking for new emoji's. The answer is, they don't. The thief is hoping that the birdwatchers and emoji seekers have reused the same username password combinations on their online banking sites, and computer sharing sites, and other more sensitive locations.

For example, in June 2016, a company called GoToMyPC had to announce that it had been "attacked." And, the result of the attack was that the company had to force all of their users to reset their passwords. That's right, after their announcement, the next time each of their users tried to use their service, the user received a message that required them to create a new password.

When this news became public, many people in the security business were surprised because GoToMyPC is one of those companies that understands enterprise security, and employs state-of-the-art technology and processes to keep their systems, and their users, safe. Also, they were part of another company called Citrix and Citrix had an excellent track record since they were founded in 1989.

So, what did GoToMyPC do wrong? What flaw existed in their enterprise security that allowed a hacker to do so much damage that the company had to force all of their users to reset their passwords?

Nothing. GoToMyPC did absolutely nothing wrong.

This was a password-reuse attack, where the attacker had successfully compiled a list of usernames and passwords from other, less secure, websites. Some of the people on that list simply used the same username and password on the GoToMyPC site. So, the attacker tried to use the usernames and passwords that he stole from another site to try to gain unauthorized access to accounts on GoToMyPC's system. Here is what the company said in a press release:

"Citrix can confirm the recent incident was a password re-use attack, where attackers used usernames and passwords leaked from other websites to access the accounts of GoToMyPC users," wrote John Bennett, product line director at Citrix. He also said that the company found no indication Citrix or its platforms have been compromised[xi].

So, GoToMyPC caught the attack early because the company is good at what they do, but not every attack ends the same way. This is why you hear the constant message from every security professional to never reuse a password. It is actually practical advice based on this common form of attack. In the habit section at the end of this chapter, you will find a suggestion on how to use different passwords on every site without driving yourself crazy.

Brute Force

Back in the 'Habit 1' chapter, you read about a method that the FBI wanted to use to break into the iPhone. It is called a brute force attack because it lacks intelligence or finesse. It is a simple trial and error program that literally attempts to try every possible combination of numbers and letters until it happens to find your password. It looks something like this:

Enter 0. If that doesn't work, try;
1. If that doesn't work, try;
2. If that doesn't work, try;
3. If that doesn't work, try;
4. If that doesn't work, try;
5. If that doesn't work, try;
6. If that doesn't work, try;
7. If that doesn't work, try;
8. If that doesn't work, try;
9. If that doesn't work, try;
a. If that doesn't work, try;
b. If that doesn't work, try;
c. If that doesn't work, try;
...and so on until:

Enter x. If that doesn't work, try;
y. If that doesn't work, try;
z. If that doesn't work, try;
A. If that doesn't work, try;
B. If that doesn't work, try;
...and so on until:

Enter X. If that doesn't work, try;
Y. If that doesn't work, try;
Z. If that doesn't work, try

At this point all of 62 possible combinations have been tried: 26 lower case letters, plus 26 upper case letter, plus ten numbers. So, a password with just one character has been ruled out. Now the computer tries the second character:

Enter 01. If that doesn't work, try;
02. if that doesn't work, try;
03. If that doesn't work, try;
...and so on until:

Enter ZX. If that doesn't work, try;
ZY. If that doesn't work, try;
ZZ. At this point, a two-character password has been ruled out, so the program tries the three-character passwords. Then 4, 5, 6, sometimes 7 character passwords are tried. In this kind of attack, 8 digits or more is not commonly tried? Why? Length of time.

If we keep the previous example of the relatively sophisticated hacker that can check 100,000,000 passwords per second, all combinations of passwords with 4 characters or less could be checked in less than 1 second.

- To check all 5 character passwords would take 9 SECONDS
- To check all 6 character passwords would take about 9 MINUTES
- To check all 7 character passwords would take almost 10 HOURS
- To check all 8 character passwords would take almost 25 DAYS.

An attack lasting 9 consecutive MINUTES is actually a long time in the world of cybersecurity; every passing second increases the chance of the attack being discovered. But, trying to maintain an attack like this for hours or days is almost impossible even on a poorly-protected site.

For comparison, here is a simple chart showing that a hacker can check 100,000 passwords a second, an Advanced Hacker that can check 100 Million per second, and a supercomputer or, more likely, a network of thousands of infected computers (also called a 'Bot-net") which are all controlled by a single thief is capable of checking 1 Billion passwords per second:

Password Characters	Simple Hacker 100 Thousand/ Sec.	Advanced Hacker 100 Million/Sec.	Super Hacker or BotNet 1 Billion/Sec.
4	2.5 Minutes	Instant	Instant
5	2.5 Hours	9 Seconds	Instant
6	6.6 Days	9.5 Mintes	57 Seconds
7	1.1 Years	9.8 Hours	1 Hour
8	69 Years	25 Days	2.5 Days
9	4,304 Years	4.3 Years	157 Days
10	266,871 Years	267 Years	26.7 Years
11	16 Million Years	16 Thousand Years	1,655 Years

Figure 13: Length of Time Needed to Crack Passwords of Varying Length

This is why you want to avoid using short passwords. Even if you memorized a completely random combination of letters and numbers, if there are fewer than seven characters, then it is almost like not having a password at all because it easy for even the least sophisticated hacker to crack.

Don't worry, the death of passwords is at hand. Really. In fact, 90% of CTO's do not believe passwords will still exist in 10 years[xii]. So, if you are reading this after the year 2026, here's hoping that you didn't have to use a login password today. What can replace it? Who knows? What we do know is that it is unlikely there will be only one type of authentication that will replace all passwords. More likely, passwords will become a combination of multiple, random, and constantly changing factors that will seek to more accurately ensure that you are who you are. Companies like AnchorID.com (The author is the CEO) and others are disrupting this market with security solutions that do not require passwords.

Habits

What's easier than writing down all of your passwords? *Not* writing them all down. Seriously.

Before you set fire to this book for the blasphemy of even suggesting that you part with your secret list of passwords, try to remember how many times the list itself has frustrated you because you either could not find it (because you hid it so well); or the password on the list did not work (because you forgot to update it); or it took you a long time to find the password you needed (because the list itself is so ridiculously long). The list itself takes time. So try not to burn this book just yet and follow these steps.

Expect this to be frustrating at first, but in time you will remember the passwords of the sites that require you to log in every day, and for the rest, it will take you about 30 seconds to log in each time. But, you can throw away your password list. If you are not ready for such a big step, then just try this method on the three sites that you are most worried about getting hacked.

This is the suggestion:

1) Set a master password on your laptop and all of your devices as discussed in Digital Habit #1: shut the front door. None of the following suggestions work otherwise.

2) Click "keep me logged in" if you have that choice on any given website.

3) Whenever you are asked for a password, and you don't remember it, don't reach for your list. Instead, click "Forgot my password." You will receive an email within a few seconds from that site. Check the sender's email address to make sure it is actually from the legitimate sender, then click the link in the email to change your password.

Reaching for the book-shredder yet? Hang in there. Remember that the light at the end of the tunnel is that you get to throw away your list of passwords. The next step is to reset your password, but before you do that remember:

- the best way to defeat the dictionary attack is to use a two-word passwords instead of one-word, and;

- to defeat a password– reuse attack, don't use the same password on more than one account, and;

- to defeat a brute force attack, use a password with 10 or more characters.

4) Set your password. OK; this is the fun part. Close your eyes. Turn your head to the left. Think of the first word that comes to mind when you open your eyes. Repeat to the right. Now, you have two random words; add a number and your done. You should end up with something like:

- clock44basket, or;
- birdsock82

Obviously, you can only do this so many times from the same desk, which may give you a reason to get up and stretch your legs for a different view during a password reset.

Again, don't try to make it easy to remember, just try to make it random words and numbers. You may find that the ridiculousness of the phrase actually makes it easy for you to remember, especially if you need to log in to that service multiple times per day.

And, voila... you have a new, secure, password that is as close as you can get to invisible, invulnerable, and invincible. Just resist the temptation to write it down to keep it as invisible as possible. If you use it often, you will remember. If not, you can use "forgot my password."

OPTIONAL: Decide if you want to use a simple password manager, or to let your Internet browser remember some of your passwords for you (most browsers will ask, do you want me to remember this password?"). Password managers are a double-edged sword; they provide additional convenience, but they give the thieves a single place to look to expose all of your passwords at once (See Digital Habit 1 - Shut the Front Door for more details). Because of that security issue, *never* add the password of your bank account or brokerage account to a password manager unless your password employs cutting-edge security, and perhaps even biometrics and geolocation.

But, using a password manager will allow you to reset your passwords only when the non-financial account forces you to do that. Keep an eye out for new password replacement technologies, or for new password managers that provide exceptional security, like optional biometrics and geolocation.

CLOSING

Now that you have read this book, you hopefully understand that simple habits, simple behaviors, simple changes can make a big difference in your ability to avoid some of the most dangerous traps set for you on the Internet. The trouble with measuring success is that you will never know about a trap that you avoided. This book will help you avoid many traps, but nothing, not even this book, will keep you completely safe from all of the traps and scams online. Neither the author nor the publisher accepts any liability whatsoever as a result of your purchasing this book and following its advice because there are just too many attacks online and they change too quickly to avoid them all. But, like a bear trap in a strip mall, it is easier to see it, and avoid it, if you know what to look for, even though many others are getting ensnared. Let this book serve as an aid to your digital life, and rest assured you will avoid more common traps with it than without it.

So, go browse the internet with more confidence and don't be afraid to try some of these habits; you will be safer, and perhaps even happier!

Glossary of Terms:

Term	***Definition***
All Writs Act of 1789	*Gives law enforcement authority to compel private companies to help carry out search warrants.*
Attack	*Any malicious act in the digital world; Online or otherwise.*
Attacker	*Anyone who intends to cause harm, or inconvenience, to others using a computer system. The motives can be rational (for example, financial gain) or irrational(just for fun) and many other reasons in between(Lake perceived activism, or political protest).*
Dark Web	*Doesn't exist. Actually a term that people in the industry tend to use to identify people who watch too much television. Here's a question: what form of material is used to physically transport most of the data you used to surf the Internet. Copper? Lithium? Nope. Glass. Fiber optics represent most of the*

	backbone of telecommunications and data systems worldwide. Fiber optics are made with a glass core because glass is a good conductor of light. And light, not electricity, carries the signal through a fiber-optic cable. So, when a fiber optic cable has been turned "on" we call that "lit." When the fiber optic cable is turned 'off,' we call it "dark." So, the term "dark web" refers to a network that has been powered off, which is not an exciting network.
Deep Web	*In general, content available in the Deep Web, is not indexed by search engines, which means you can't find this content through Google. The owners of this content do not want to be found unless you know where to look. You need to know a specific IP address, or URL, to find them. Over 84% of all Internet content is in the deep web; the other 16%*[xiii] *is accessible through Standard search engines like Google. The Deep Web is what people are commonly referring to when they use the term "dark web."*

	Other names include Hidden Web, Deep Net, Invisible Net, Invisible Web. [ENDNOTE: http://www.deepweb-sites.com/]
Device	*Any electronic device that can connect to the internet, including: laptops, desktops, smartphones, tablets, mobile 'flip' phones, etcetera.*
Digital Life	*The time you spend interacting with any computerized device that is connected to a network. This includes laptops, desktops, workstations, mobile phones, tablets, televisions, MP3 (music) players, etc. Basically anything with a chip in it, and the ability for you to interact with it. For the purpose of this book, habits around interaction with devices that are only connected to the "Internet of Things" or IOT.*
Encrypted	*The use of a process, or software, that masks Digital content. The content is typically unmasked with a key, or secret code.*
Hack	*To manage successfully.*

Hacker	*Anyone who finds their way around the intended use of the system. For the purpose of this book, all ' hacker' activity is malicious.*
Hopelessly Encrypted	*This typically refers to an encryption method called AES 256 Kb, which essentially is a string of 256 ones and zeros. How long would it take to decrypt a string of 256 ones and zeros if you do not know the correct order? A strong computer can do about 2 billion calculations in a second. Imagine you could somehow connect 1 billion of these computers together working on the same problem at the same time. If such a computer could be built, it would take that computer approximately seven times longer than the universe has existed (The universe has been around for about 14 billion years) and it would require the power consumption of 150 nuclear power plants.*
Internet of Things	*For the purpose of this book, items such as toasters, refrigerators, and remote cameras that connect through the internet to another*

	computer, but are not designed for direct integration with the user. For contrast, a laptop is specifically designed for interaction with the user, a toaster is not.
Secure Enclave	*A portion of the hardware in an iPhone that is used to store a 256 kb encrypted key, which is a unique identifier for each iPhone.*
Sleep Mode	*A operational mode for a computer or mobile device in which the device does not function, and the display screen appears to be 'off.' This is designed to save energy without actually turning the device off. When a laptop or other device goes into sleep mode, it typically saves everything you are doing in every program or app that is open at the time that Sleep Mode begins. The main advantage is that Sleep mode requires much less power usage than when the computer is fully operating, The computer isn't exactly off, and it restores itself quickly, as opposed to actually turning the device completely powered off because that takes more*

	time to restore the device than sleep mode. Also known as 'Stand By' Mode or' Suspend' mode,
SSID	*Service Set Identifier. This is the 'name' of a Wi-Fi network.*
Stand By Mode	*See "Sleep Mode"*
Surface Web	*The approximately 16% of Internet content that is indexed, and searchable, through standard search engines like Google and Yahoo.*
Suspend Mode	*See "Sleep Mode"*
System Password	*A password, or numeric passcode, that is required before a device will turn 'on' after either being turned 'off' or after entering 'sleep mode.'*
Thief	*Anyone who intends to steal from you. In the context of this book, "Thief," Is someone who is trying to use a computer or mobile device to steal from you.*
User	*A person with a heartbeat and a Digital Life.*

About the Author

David W. Schropfer is the CEO of AnchorID, Incorporated, a cybersecurity company in New York (www.AnchorID.com). Every day, he and his team of professionals keep the people who use AnchorID safe from some of the most common traps, hacks and attacks that target computer systems of all sizes.

David's previous books include The Smartphone Wallet, and three industry whitepapers, which predicted some of the biggest trends in the payments, mobile, and security industries.

Since graduating Boston College, David earned an Executive MBA from the University of Miami.

End Notes

[i] Excerpt from Mirriam Webster dictionary, 2016.

[ii]http://www.hackmageddon.com/category/security/cyber-attacks-statistics/

[iii] https://preyproject.com/blog/2013/03/prey-labs-these-are-places-your-stolen-laptop-will-most-likely-end-up-at

[iv] https://en.wikipedia.org/wiki/2015_San_Bernardino_attack

[v] http://www.apple.com/customer-letter/

[vi] FCC Document: https://apps.fcc.gov/edocs_public/attachmatch/FCC-16-39A1.pdf

[vii] http://krebsonsecurity.com/2013/06/the-value-of-a-hacked-email-account/

[viii] http://honan.net

[ix] https://apps.fcc.gov/edocs_public/attachmatch/FCC-16-39A1.pdf

[x] http://www.lockdown.co.uk/?pg=combi&s=articles

[xi] http://status.gotomypc.com/incidents/s2k8h1xhzn4k

[xii] http://www.infosecurity-magazine.com/news/passwords-will-be-eliminated/

[xii] http://www.deepweb-sites.com

www.ingramcontent.com/pod-product-compliance
Lightning Source LLC
Chambersburg PA
CBHW031224050326
40689CB00009B/1460
9781535297998